Cooking with *Lil Mama*

By
Tonja Nelson

Disclaimer

Dedication

This book is dedicated in loving memory of my
Grandmother Mary L. Hodges

LIL Mama's Catering LLC

LIL Mama's Catering LLC, led by owner Tonja Stewart Nelson, stands as a beacon of culinary excellence in the heart of Victorville, California. Tonja's passion for soul food and Hispanic cuisine infuses every aspect of our operations. Rooted in Southern traditions and inspired by Latin flavors, our menu offerings promise a delightful fusion of taste and authenticity.

From intimate gatherings to large-scale events, our mobile catering service brings the flavors of the South and Hispanic cuisine directly to our customers' doorsteps. With a commitment to community engagement and a deep-seated desire to make a positive impact, we strive to exceed expectations and leave a lasting impression on every individual we serve.

Driven by a dedication to culinary innovation and a relentless pursuit of excellence, LIL Mama's Catering LLC continues to be a trusted choice for those seeking flavorful, memorable dining experiences.

Lil Mama's Catering LLC, a premier catering service specializing in soul food and Hispanic cuisine. Founded by Tonja Stewart Nelson, a seasoned chef with over 12 years of culinary experience, our company is dedicated to providing exceptional quality and service to the public.

With roots deeply embedded in Southern cooking traditions, Tonja's upbringing in Mobile, Alabama, instilled in her a profound passion for food from an early age. Guided by her grandmother's teachings and armed with a blend of traditional flavors and modern techniques, Tonja has crafted a menu that not only tantalizes taste buds but also delights the eyes with its visual appeal.

At LIL Mama's Catering LLC, we pride ourselves on our commitment to excellence and our unwavering dedication to our community. Beyond simply delivering delicious meals, we strive to make a positive impact by actively participating in charitable endeavors and supporting those in need.

Serving Los Angeles, Victorville, Hesperia, and Adelanto, our mobile catering service brings the flavors of the South and Hispanic cuisine directly to your doorstep. In a competitive landscape dominated by food trucks, we stand out with our authentic flavors, impeccable service, and a genuine passion for culinary excellence.

Mission Statement

Our mission is to provide a memorable culinary experience that celebrates the rich flavors of Southern and Hispanic cuisine while delivering exceptional quality and service to our customers.

Vision Statement

Our vision is to become the premier destination for soul food and Hispanic cuisine, recognized for our unwavering commitment to quality, innovation, and community engagement. We aspire to expand our reach while staying true to our roots, continually delighting our customers with our flavorful creations and leaving a lasting impression on every community we serve.

Cooking with Lil Mama

Lil Mama's Baked Salmon & Asparagus

2 servings   15 minutes

INGREDIENTS

- 1 ½ pounds of Salmon cut in four filets.
- 2 tablespoons of Parsley
- 2 tablespoons of Extra Virgin Olive Oil
- 2 tablespoons of Lemon Juice
- 3 Cloves of Garlic
- ½ tablespoons of Dijon Mustard
- ½ teaspoons of Black Pepper
- ½ of Lemon sliced into four rings

DIRECTIONS

- Preheat oven to 450°F (230°C).
- Cover a baking pan with a 12-14 inch piece of foil.
- In a small bowl, combine chopped parsley, pressed garlic cloves, olive oil, lemon juice, Dijon mustard, salt, and pepper.
- Wash the asparagus and cut off the tough ends. Drizzle the asparagus with olive oil.
- Place the salmon on the foil-covered pan.
- Cover the salmon and asparagus with the garnish mixture.
- Make sure both the salmon and asparagus are well covered with foil.
- Bake in the preheated oven for about 15-20 minutes, or until the salmon is cooked through and the asparagus is tender.
- Serve and enjoy!

| SERVINGS: 2 | PREPPING TIME: 15 MIN | COOKING TIME: 30 MIN |

INGREDIENTS

- 3 Pounds of Sweet Potatoes
- ½ cup of Unsalted Butter
- 2 tablespoons of Heavy
- Cream
- ¾ cup of packed Light
- Brown Sugar
- ½ teaspoon of Ground
- Cinnamon
- ½ teaspoon of grated
- Nutmeg
- ½ teaspoon of Salt
- 2 cups of Sugar

DIRECTIONS

- Preheat oven to 350 degrees, light butter a baking dish. Peel sweet potatoes, slice them into ½ inch thick circles, place the slices in buttered baking dish.

- In a medium saucepan heat the butter and heavy cream over a medium heat until butter is melted and hot. In another sauce pan combine brown sugar,

- Cinnamon, nutmeg and salt, pour melted butter over the mixture and stir well.

- Pour the mixture over the potatoes until completely coated, cover the dish with aluminum foil.

- Bake for 25 minutes, remove the foil and gently stir.

- Leave sweet potatoes uncovered baking them for an additional 30 minutes until tender and syrupy.

  Enjoy!!

Lil Mama's Cajun Chicken Gumbo

INGREDIENTS

- 2 pounds of Skinless, Boneless Chicken Thighs
- 2 ½ teaspoons of Cajun Seasoning
- ½ teaspoon of Garlic Powder
- 1 cup of Vegetable Oil Divided
- 1 pound of Andouille Sausage, cut into pieces.
- 1 ½ cup of All Purpose Flour
- 1 large White Onion finely chopped.
- 1 large Green Bell Pepper seeded and chopped.
- 1 Pepper Jalapeno Pepper seeded and chopped.
- 2 Stalks of Celery finely chopped.

- 3 Cloves of minced Garlic
- 1 teaspoon of Kosher Salt
- 6 cups of Chicken Stock
- 2 Bay Leaves
- 1 teaspoon of Black Pepper
- 1 tablespoon of Worcestershire Sauce
- 2 teaspoons of Hot Sauce
- ½ pound of sliced Okra
- 4 cups of White Rice

DIRECTIONS

- Sliced green Onion for the top as garnish.
- Preheat oven to 325°F (160°C).
- Place chicken in a baking dish and bake for about 50-60 minutes until no longer pink inside.
- Allow the chicken to cool down and set it aside.
- Put about 2 teaspoons of oil into a pan, add sausage, and cook for about 3-5 minutes or until golden brown.
- Remove sausage and drain on a paper towel, reserving drippings in the pan.
- In the same pan, add flour, brown, and stir often until the roux is a dark brown color.

- Once the roux is dark brown, add onions, peppers, celery, garlic, and salt.
- Increase to medium heat and cook for 5 minutes, stirring constantly until vegetables are tender.
- Stir in remaining seasonings and bring to a boil, stirring occasionally.
- Reduce heat to medium-low, add reserved chicken, sausage, and okra, and simmer for 20 minutes.
- Serve over rice and top with green onions.

  Enjoy!

Lil Mama's Baked Fried Chicken

INGREDIENTS

- 8 to 10 Pieces of Chicken (pieces of your choice)
- 1 cup of All Purpose Flour
- ½ teaspoon of Salt
- 1 tablespoon of Seasoning Salt (my preference Lawry's)
- ¾ teaspoon of Pepper
- 2 teaspoons of Paprika
- ½ stick or ¼ cup of Butter
- 2 cups of Buttermilk
- 1 gallon or 2 pieces Lock bag

2 servings   15 minutes

DIRECTIONS

- Place chicken pieces in buttermilk one piece at a time, cover, and let marinate for 30-40 minutes.

- Combine flour, salt, seasoning salt, pepper, and paprika in a Ziplock bag or large bowl, and mix thoroughly.

- Cut ½ a stick of butter into a few pieces and place them in a 13-inch pan.

- Melt the butter in the oven.

- Spread the melted butter in the bottom of the pan and lightly spray with cooking oil spray, ensuring there are no dry spots.

- Shake excess buttermilk off the chicken and coat each piece in the combined seasonings, shaking well until completely coated.

- Place each coated piece into the pan.

- Bake at 375°F (190°C) for 20 minutes on each side, longer for larger pieces of chicken.

- Once cooked to your liking, drain off any extra oil.

  Serve and enjoy!

Lil Mama's Buffalo Lemon Peppered Wings

INGREDIENTS

- 1 pound of Chicken Wings
- 2 tablespoons of Lemon Garlic Seasoning
- 1 tablespoon of Pepper
- 1 tablespoon of Avocado Oil

DIRECTIONS

- Season the wings liberally with the lemon garlic seasoning and pepper, toss with 1 tablespoon of avocado oil.

AIR FRYER:

- Place the wings in the air fryer at 360 degrees for 15 minutes. Finish the wings on 400 degrees for 4 – 5 minutes, this will make them have a perfect outside crust. Toss the wings in the sauce.

Oven:

- Preheat the oven to 435 degrees. Place the wings on a foil line baking sheet. Make sure there is ample enough space between each wing. Use a second sheet pan if needed. Bake for 10 minutes, bake on each - side for 10 extra minutes. Toss the wings in the sauce and bake for an extra 5 minutes, squeeze a fresh lemon on top.

Wing Sauce

- ¾ cups of Franks Red Hot Sauce
- 2 tablespoons of Ghee
- 1 tablespoon of Apple Cider Vinegar

- In a small sauce pan combine Frank's Red Hot Sauce, Ghee, and Apple Cider Vinegar, bring to a simmer and turn the heat off. Serve with juice of ½ lemon.Enjoy!

Lil Mama's
Crock Pot Beef Stew

INGREDIENTS

- 2 tablespoons of Oil
- 1.5 pounds of Beef stewing meat in chucks
- 1 ½ teaspoons of Salt or less
- 1 ½ of Black Pepper to taste
- 2 tablespoons of Flour
- 1 Green Bell pepper
- 1 Orange Bell pepper
- 1 Yellow Bell Pepper

DIRECTIONS

Gravy

- 2 large Yellow Onions cut into wedges.
- 2 cloves of Garlic sliced.
- 2 tablespoons of Italian seasoning
- 4 tablespoons of Tomato Paste
- ½ cup of red Wine or use more stock
- 2 cups of Beef Stock
- 2 tablespoons of Worcestershire Sauce
- 1 tablespoon of Maple Syrup

Vegetables

- 3 large Waxy Potatoes or Red Skin Potatoes
- 4 large Carrots peeled and cut into chunks.
- 4 large Celery sticks trimmed and sliced.
- ½ cup of frozen Peas

- Heat Oil in a large and deep skillet over medium – high heat. In a small bowl mix in beef cubes, salt, flour (small amount to cover meat) and pepper. Stir well, then add to hot oil cook until beef is brown on both sides DO NOT stir too much or beef will not brown properly. Remove the beef, add it to 5 – 6-quart slow cooker.

Gravy:

- Put the skillet back on the stove at medium – high heat,

add a little more oil. Cook the onions and garlic until softens, add in all three bell peppers, Italian seasoning and tomato paste. Stirring constantly for 1 minute until the herbs are fragrant. Pour in red wine and cook for 1 minute. Stir in beef stock, Worcestershire sauce and maple syrup. Bring to a boil, this will help the stew to start cooking faster, transfer to slow cooker.

On top of the meat place carrots, potatoes, celery, and remaining bell peppers. Pour the hot liquid from the skillet into the crockpot making the liquid run down to the bottom and underneath the meat. Cook the stew for 8 hours on low or 4 hours on high, 10 minutes before cooking is done add in the frozen peas. Finish cooking with the lid open if you want a thick stew or cook with the lid closed if you want more of a soupier look. Enjoy!

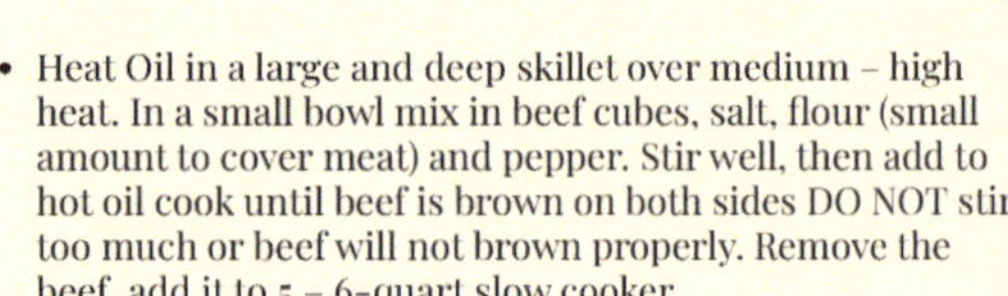

Lil Mama's
Deep Fried Southern Red Snapper

INGREDIENTS

- 1 Lemon
- 2 pounds of Red Snapper
- 2 Eggs, lightly beaten.
- ½ cup of Yellow Mustard
- 1 tablespoon Creole or Cajun Seasoning

- 1/3 cup of Heavy Cream or Milk
- 1 cup of Cornmeal
- ½ cup of Flour
- 1 tablespoon of Blackened Seasoning

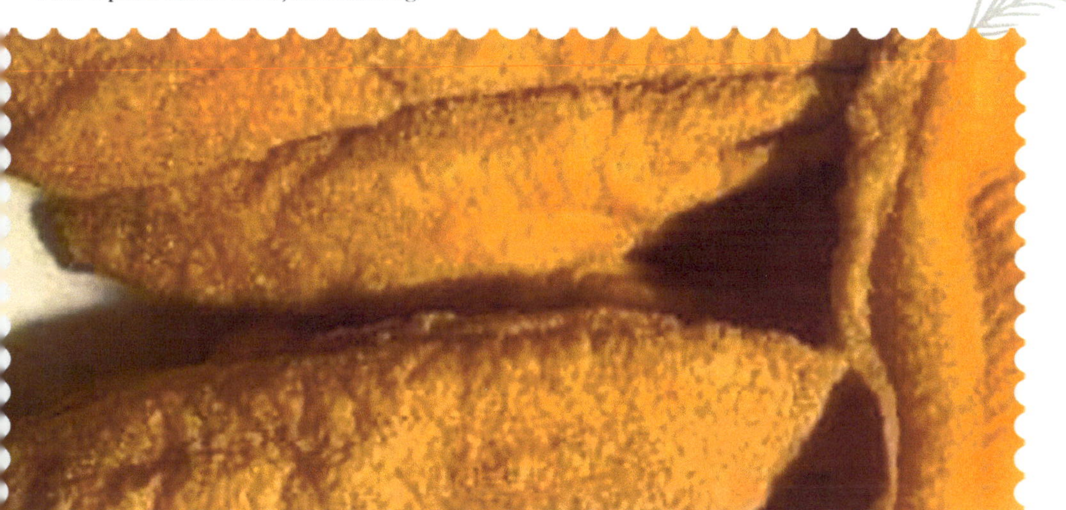

DIRECTIONS

- In a Ziploc bag, add cornmeal, flour, creole seasoning, and blackened seasoning, then set aside.
- In a bowl, mix together egg and milk or heavy cream.
- Lightly coat the fish in mustard.
- Dip the mustard-coated fish pieces into the egg wash.
- Place the fish pieces into the Ziploc bag with the dry mixture, seal, and shake to coat evenly.
- Heat oil to 350°F (175°C).
- Fry the fish in the hot oil until they are golden brown.
- Remove the fish and sprinkle a small amount of creole and blackened seasoning on top.
- Enjoy!

Lil Mama's
Gumbo Collard Greens

INGREDIENTS

- Smoked Turkey Leg
- Sweet Onion
- 7 bunches of Collard Greens
- ½ cup of Vinegar
- ½ cup of Brown Sugar
- 3 tablespoons of Collard Greens seasoning
- 2 tablespoons of Chicken Bouillon base or powder
- ½ cup of Red Bell Pepper
- ½ cup of Green Bell Pepper
- 2 tablespoons of Banana Peppers
- ½ cup of Olive Oil
- 1 pound of Shrimp
- ½ pound of Andouille Sausage
- ½ cup of Okra
- ½ cup of celery

DIRECTIONS

- Combine onions, bell peppers, celery, and olive oil in a pot.
- Simmer on low until vegetables are tender, then set aside.
- In a large pot, cook the turkey leg for about 30 to 40 minutes.
- Add in collard greens and cook for 2 to 4 hours until tender.
- Add in sausage, shrimp, okra, and the cooked vegetables.
- Cook for another 20 minutes or until the greens are tender to your liking.
- Enjoy!

Lil Mama's Homemade Banana Pudding

INGREDIENTS

- 1 cup of Sugar
- 3 Eggs beaten
- 1 dash of Salt
- 2 tablespoons of Cornstarch
- 2 cups of Milk
- ½ teaspoon of Vanilla Extract
- 1 tablespoon of Bourbon
- 3-4 ripe Bananas sliced.
- Vanilla Wafers
- Whipped Cream for topping

DIRECTIONS

- Combine sugar, eggs, salt, cornstarch, and milk in a saucepan.
- Bring the mixture to a boil over medium-high heat, stirring constantly.
- Cook until thickened, ensuring to stir constantly from the beginning.
- Remove from heat and add vanilla extract and bourbon for flavor.
- In a 9-inch square casserole dish, layer wafers, bananas, and pudding, repeating until the top of the dish is reached.
- Alternatively, layer the pudding in 6 individual-sized glass jars or ice cream bowls.
- Top with whipped cream.
- Enjoy!

SERVINGS: 2   PREPPING TIME: 15 MIN   COOKING TIME: 30 MIN

INGREDIENTS

- ½ cup of Sugar
- ½ tablespoon of Oil
- 4 Eggs
- 1 pinch of Salt
- 1 tablespoon of Baking Powder
- 1 pinch of Baking Soda
- 1 cup of All Purpose Flour
- ½ cup of Milk
- 1 tablespoon of Vanilla Extract
- 1 tablespoon of grated Lemon
- 2 tablespoons of fresh lemon Juice
- ½ cup of Icing Sugar
- 1 cup of chilled Whipping Cream

DIRECTIONS

- In a bowl, add sugar and oil, beat for 2 minutes.
- Add 4 eggs, one by one, beating well after each addition.
- Add a pinch of salt, 1 tablespoon of baking powder, and a pinch of baking soda. Mix well.
- Gradually add 1 cup of all-purpose flour, mixing after each addition.
- Lastly, add ½ cup of milk and mix until combined.
- Stir in 1 tablespoon of vanilla extract, 1 tablespoon of lemon juice, and 1 tablespoon of grated lemon zest.
- Grease a pan with butter or oil.
- Pour the mixture into the pan.
- Bake at 325°F (160°C) for 30-35 minutes.
- In a bowl, add ½ cup icing sugar and 1 cup of chilled whipped cream. Beat until soft.

Lil Mama's Famous Collard Greens

INGREDIENTS

- Smoked Ham hock or Neckbones
- 1 sweet Onion
- 7 bunches of Collard Greens
- ½ cup of Vinegar
- ½ cup of Brown Sugar
- 2 teaspoons of Chicken Bouillon base or powder

- 3 tablespoons of Collard Green seasoning
- 2 teaspoons of Banana peppers
- 2 teaspoons of Red Pepper Flakes
- ½ cup of Olive Oil
- 1 teaspoon of Paprika
- 2 teaspoons of Lawry's seasoning

DIRECTIONS

- Combine oil, onions, and smoked ham hock in a pot.
- Stir for 5 minutes, then add chicken stock.
- Cook for about an hour or until the meat is very tender.
- Add collard greens, brown sugar, vinegar, and all seasonings.
- Cook for 2 to 3 hours or until the greens are tender to your liking.
- Remove the bones.
- Enjoy!

Lil Mama's
Green Beans

DIRECTIONS

- Heat olive oil in a Dutch oven over medium heat.

- Sauté onions until softened, about 3 to 5 minutes.

- Add green beans, Lipton onion soup pack, and seasonings.

- Pour in enough chicken broth to cover the green beans.

- Bring to a boil, then reduce heat and simmer for 30 minutes.

- Add potatoes and cook for another 20 minutes or until potatoes are tender.

- Enjoy!

INGREDIENTS

- 1 to 2 pounds of Green Beans

- All-purpose seasoning (to taste)

- ½ cup of Chicken Broth

- 8 Red Potatoes

- ½ teaspoon of crushed Red Pepper Flakes

- 1 package of Lipton Onion Soup mix

- 1 chopped Onion

- ½ teaspoon of Rosemary Flakes

- ½ teaspoon of Olive Oil

Lil Mama's Lobster Tail w/ Garlic Butter Sauce

INGREDIENTS

- 2 large Lobster Tails
- 4 tablespoons of Unsalted Butter
- 3 cloves of Garlic
- 1 teaspoon of Paprika (smoked)
- ½ teaspoon of Salt
- ½ teaspoon of Black Pepper
- 1 tablespoon of Lemon Juice
- 1 tablespoon of fresh Parsley
- Lemon Wedges (for serving)

DIRECTIONS

- Use kitchen shears to cut along the middle of the top of the lobster tail.
- Loosen the shell halves apart and use a spoon or fingertip to loosen the lobster meat.
- Pull the meat completely out, leaving the tail part still attached.
- Close the shell part back together and arrange the meat on top of the shell.
- Place the prepared lobster tails on a lined baking rack.
- Position the rack in the oven 4-6 inches from the heat source.
- Cook in the oven for about 6 minutes, or approximately 1 minute for every ounce of lobster meat.

Butter Sauce Ingredients

- 1 ½ stick of Butter
- ½ cup of Parmesan Cheese
- ½ teaspoon of Garlic Salt
- 1 teaspoon of Parsley
- 1 clove of minced Garlic
- ¼ cup of Mozzarella Cheese

- Put the ingredients for the butter sauce in a saucepan.
- Simmer until all the ingredients are combined and melted.
- Garnish the lobster tail with the butter sauce.
- Enjoy!

Lil Mama's
Mac & Cheese

INGREDIENTS

- 16 oz of large Elbow Pasta
- 2 Eggs
- 8 oz Sour Cream
- 1 cup of Milk
- 1 stick of Butter
- 1 teaspoon of Paprika
- Season Salt to taste
- 1 teaspoon of Black Pepper
- Cheddar Cheese
- Extra Sharp Cheddar Cheese
- Colby Cheese

DIRECTIONS

- Preheat oven to 350°F (175°C).
- Boil noodles according to the directions on the back of the box.
- Shred your choice of cheese.
- Transfer the cooked noodles to a large mixing bowl.
- Add 1 stick of butter to the noodles.
- In a separate bowl, whisk together eggs, sour cream, and seasonings.
- Slowly mix in shredded cheese and other cheeses.
- Spray a baking dish with oil or butter.
- Add the macaroni mixture to the baking dish.
- Bake for 45 minutes.
- Remove from oven and add more cheese on top.
- Bake for an additional 5 minutes until golden on top.
- Enjoy!

Lil Mama's Short Ribs

INGREDIENTS

- 4-6 Beef Short Ribs (meaty)
- 1 tablespoon of Oil
- 1 pealed and sliced Onion
- 3 Garlic cloves peeled and chopped
- 1 mug 240 ml of Red Wine
- 2 ¾ cups of Vegeable Bouillon

- 2 cups of Water
- 1 tablespoon of Dry Thyme
- 1 tablespoon of Tomato puree or paste
- 1 teaspoon of Sugar
- ½ teaspoon of Salt
- ¼ tablespoon of Worcestershire Sauce

DIRECTIONS

Gravy

- 2 tablespoons of Flour or Cornstarch
- 5 tablespoons of Water
- 1 tablespoon of Oil
- In a large skillet, heat oil.
- Brown the short ribs on both sides in the skillet, about 4 to 5 minutes on each side.

- Add onion and garlic to the skillet.
- Briefly start adding the red wine, then add remaining ingredients.
- Bring to a boil, then reduce to low heat and continue cooking for 2 to 4 minutes.
- Transfer all ingredients to a stew pot.
- Cook for about 6 to 8 hours with the lid on.

Lil Mama's Shrimp & Bacon Bake Potato

INGREDIENTS

- 3 to 4 Potatoes
- Ginger
- 6 slices of Bacon
- Sour Cream
- Green Onions
- Cheddar Cheese
- Shrimp
- Butter

DIRECTIONS

- Wash the potatoes and wrap them in aluminum foil.
- Bake at 450°F (230°C) for about 1 ½ hours, adjusting the time as needed based on the size of the potatoes.
- Unwrap the potatoes and cut them down the middle.
- In a skillet, sauté shrimp in butter and ginger.
- Add butter, cheese, green onions, shrimp, bacon, and sour cream to the top of the potatoes.
- Enjoy!

Lil Mama's Southern Cabbage

INGREDIENTS

- ½ teaspoon of Olive Oil
- 1 chopped Onion
- 1 chopped Cabbage
- ½ stick of Butter
- ½ teaspoon of Salt
- ½ teaspoon of Pepper
- ½ teaspoon of Lawry's seasoning
- ½ teaspoon of Garlic Salt
- 6 slices of Bacon

DIRECTIONS

- Add olive oil to a pan over medium heat.

- In a separate pan, fry bacon cut into pieces until crispy, then set aside.

- Cook onions in the olive oil until soft and translucent.

- Add cabbage and butter to the pan, cooking until the cabbage wilts.

- Stir in the cooked bacon.

- Season with garlic salt and seasoning salt to taste.

- Enjoy!

Lil Mama's Southern Oxtail Soup

INGREDIENTS

- 2 to 3 pounds of Oxtails
- ½ teaspoon of Olive Oil
- ¼ cup of Brown Sugar
- 2 teaspoons of Worcestershire Sauce
- 1 chopped Onion
- 2 chopped Green Onions
- 1 teaspoon of smoked Paprika
- 1 whole Scotch Bonnet Pepper
- 1 can of Tomato paste
- 1 pound of Carrots
- 4 Red Potatoes cut into squares
- 1 can of Corn
- 1 ½ stalks of Celery cut into small pieces
- Seasoning Salt
- Black Pepper
- 1 ½ teaspoons of Garlic Powder
- ½ cup of Flour
- 2 cups of Beef Stock

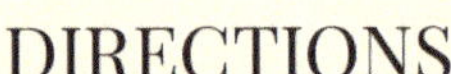

DIRECTIONS

- Brown oxtails in olive oil, then cover them with seasoned flour.
- In a slow cooker, combine beef stock, brown sugar, Worcestershire sauce, onions, smoked paprika, and tomato paste.
- Bring the mixture to a boil, then add oxtails.
- Add two cups of water, cover, and cook for 7 to 8 hours.
- In the last hour of cooking, add potatoes, corn, and carrots.
- Cook for an additional hour.
- Serve the dish over a bed of rice.
- Enjoy!

Lil Mama's Hennessy Shrimp

INGREDIENTS

- 1 pound of Shrimp
- ½ cup of Hennessy
- ½ stick of Butter
- 1 tablespoon of Cajun Seasoning
- 2 tablespoons of Brown Swerve or Brown Sugar substitute
- ½ tablespoon minced Garlic
- ½ tablespoon of Red Pepper Flakes
- 1 teaspoon of Onion Powder
- White Pepper or Black Pepper to taste
- Parsley
- ½ tablespoons of Blackened Seasoning

DIRECTIONS

- Clean and devein the shrimp, then season them with your choice of white or black pepper, onion powder, Cajun seasoning, and blackened seasoning. Set aside.

- Melt butter on high heat in a pan, then add minced garlic.

- Toss the seasoned shrimp in the pan and cook on both sides for 4-5 minutes or until they turn pink.

- Pour Hennessy into the pan and continue to toss the shrimp. If the pan begins to smoke, it's just the alcohol burning off. Continue cooking.

- Add brown Swerve or your choice of brown sugar, and crushed red pepper flakes.

- Keep tossing the shrimp, coating them in the Hennessy sauce as it thickens.

- Remove the shrimp from the pan and garnish with parsley.

- Enjoy!

Lil Mama's Lemon Blueberry Loaf

INGREDIENTS

- 1 ½ cup plus 1 tablespoon of All Purpose Flour
- 2 teaspoons of Baking Powder
- 3 large Eggs
- 1 cup of plain Yogurt or Sour Cream
- ½ teaspoon of Salt 
- ½ teaspoon of Vanilla Extract
- ½ cup of Vegetable Oil
- 2 teaspoons of Lemon Zest
- 1 ½ cup fresh or frozen Blueberries

🍴 2 servings   🕐 15 minutes

Lemon Glaze Syrup 

- 2 to 3 tablespoons of Lemon Juice
- 1 cup of sifted confectioners' Sugar

DIRECTIONS

- Preheat the oven to 350 degrees and grease the sides and bottom of a pan.
- Mix all the dry ingredients for the bread in a bowl.
- In a large bowl, add the tablespoon of flour to the blueberries and fold gently into the batter.
- Pour the batter into the prepared pan and bake for 50 to 55 minutes.
- Use a toothpick to check if the bread is baked all the way through. If it comes out clean, the bread is done.
- In a small saucepan on low heat, simmer lemon juice and powdered sugar for 3 minutes until dissolved.
- Poke holes in the bread with a toothpick and use a pastry brush to brush on the glaze.
- Let the glaze harden for 15 minutes before serving.
- Enjoy!

Lil Mama's Fried Chicken Strips

INGREDIENTS

- 8 to 10 pieces of Chicken cut into strips.
- 1 ½ cup of Cornstarch
- ¼ cup of Flour
- 1 tablespoon of Paprika
- 1 ½ tablespoon of Onion Powder
- 1 ¾ teaspoon of Salt
- ½ teaspoon of Black Pepper
- 1 teaspoon of Baking Soda
- ½ teaspoon of Baking Powder
- ¾ cups of Water
- 3 cups of Peanut Oil
- 2 teaspoons of Seasoning Salt
- 2 teaspoons of Cayenne Pepper
- 2 teaspoons of Creole Seasoning

DIRECTIONS

- In a bowl, mix cornstarch, flour, paprika, onion powder, black pepper, baking soda, baking powder, seasoning salt, cayenne pepper, and creole seasoning.
- Add water and whisk until combined.
- Put ¼ cup of cornstarch in a shallow pan.
- Coat the chicken in the cornstarch.
- Dip the coated chicken into the wet batter until completely coated, letting excess drip off for a couple of seconds.
- In a pot filled with peanut oil, fry the chicken at 350 degrees for 8 to 10 minutes until cooked through, in small batches.
- Drain the fried chicken on a metal rack.
- Sprinkle some creole seasoning on top.
- Enjoy!

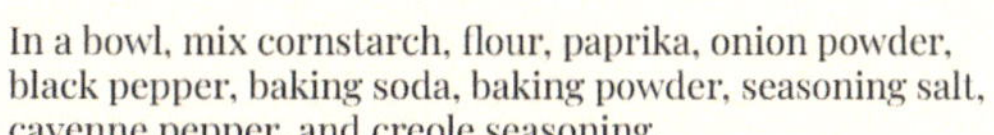

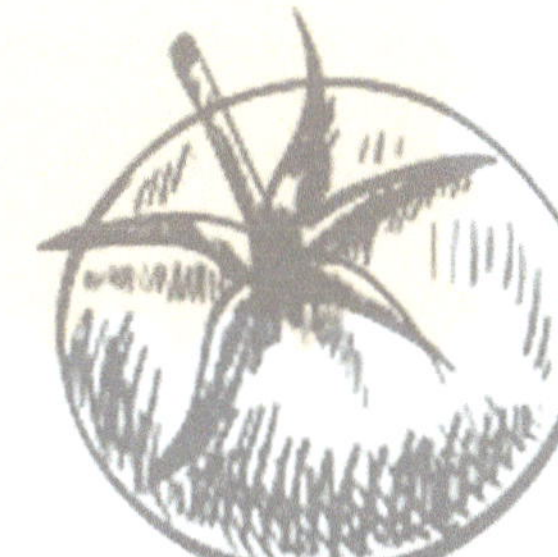

Lil Mama's Banana Pudding Cheesecake Squares

INGREDIENTS

- ½ cup of unsalted Butter melted
- ½ cup of light Brown Sugar packed
- 1 large Egg Yolk
- ½ cup of All Purpose Flour
- Pinch of Salt
- ¼ cup of mashed ripe Bananas
- 1 teaspoon of Pure Vanilla Extract

DIRECTIONS

Cheesecake Topping

- 2/3 cup of Heavy Whipped Cream
- 16 ounces Cream Cheese (2 blocks)
- 1 cup of Sugar
- 3.4 ounces of instant Banana pudding powder
- ½ cup of Milk
- 1 teaspoon of Vanilla Extract
- Garnish Nilla Wafers

Lil Mama's Peach Cobbler

INGREDIENTS

- 10 fresh Peaches – peeled, pitted, and sliced.
- ½ cup plus 2 tablespoons of Butter cut into pieces
- 2 ½ cups of All Purpose Flour
- ½ cup plus 2 teaspoons of Brown Sugar
- 2 ½ cups of white Sugar
- 2 ½ teaspoons of Baking Powder
- 1 ½ teaspoons of Salt
- 3 Eggs lightly beaten.
- 1 ½ cups of Vegetable Oil
- 1 tablespoon of Ground Cinnamon
- 1 pack of Puffy Pastry

DIRECTIONS

- Bake the pastry as directed and set aside to cool. Once cooled, break it into pieces.
- Preheat the oven to 350 degrees. Spray a 9 x 13-inch baking pan with cooking spray (butter spray) and layer puff pastry into the bottom of the pan.
- Arrange the peaches on top of the puff pastry, then place the butter pieces on top of the peaches. Sprinkle brown sugar evenly on top and set aside.
- In a mixing bowl, mix flour, sugar, baking powder, and salt together.
- Beat the oil and eggs together, then stir them into the dry mixture.
- Evenly spread the batter on top of the peaches, covering the entire top.
- Sprinkle cinnamon on top.
- Place in the oven for about 50 minutes to an hour.
- Let it cool, then enjoy with vanilla ice cream on top.
- Enjoy!

Lil Mama's
Shrimp Scampi

INGREDIENTS

- 3 to 4 cloves of minced Garlic
- 1 ¼ up of Butter cubed.
- ¼ cup of Olive Oil
- 1 pound of uncooked Shrimp peeled.
- ¼ cup of Lemon Juice
- ½ teaspoon Pepper
- ¼ teaspoon of dried Oregano
- ½ cup of grated Parmesan Cheese
- ½ cup of fresh Parsley
- 1 box of Angel Hair Pasta

DIRECTIONS

- In a pot, boil 3 cups of water. Add angel hair pasta and cook for about 4 to 5 minutes.

- In a skillet, sauté garlic in butter and oil for about 2 minutes.

- Add shrimp to the skillet and cook until they turn a light pink color.

- Stir in lemon juice, pepper, and oregano.

- Serve the cooked angel hair pasta on plates, and top with the shrimp and sauce.

- Enjoy!

Lil Mama's Spaghetti w/ Ground Beef & Sauce

INGREDIENTS

- 1 ½ pounds of Ground Beef
- 1 ½ teaspoon of Salt
- ½ teaspoon of Black Pepper
- 1 ½ up of Onion
- 1 small Green Bell Pepper
- 1 small Red Bell Pepper
- 1 tablespoon of Garlic
- ½ Purple Onion
- 1 28 ounce can of Tomatoes (crushed)
- 1 32 ounce can of Prego Sauce
- 1 6 ounce can of Tomato Paste
- 1 tablespoon of Italian Seasoning
- 1 ½ tablespoon of Parsley (dried)
- 16 ounces of Spaghetti Noodles
- 1 cup of Parmesan Cheese
- 1 cup of Cheddar Cheese

DIRECTIONS

- Brown the ground beef in a skillet until cooked through, then set aside.
- Sauté bell peppers, garlic, and onion in the skillet. Add sauce to the pan and simmer for about 10 minutes.
- In a large pot, boil the spaghetti noodles for 7-8 minutes until tender, then drain the water.
- Add the cooked spaghetti noodles to the skillet with the sautéed vegetables and spaghetti sauce.
- Mix everything well and transfer to a baking dish.
- Bake in the oven for about 25 minutes.
- Remove from the oven and top with cheese, then bake for an additional 2 to 3 minutes until the cheese is melted.
- Let cool for 10 minutes before serving.
- Enjoy!

Lil Mama's Southern Homemade Chilli

INGREDIENTS

- 1 pound of Ground Beef
- 1 pound of Hot Sausage
- 3 tablespoons of Chili Powder
- 2 stalks of Celery
- 1 medium Onion
- 1 medium Red Bell Pepper
- 1 medium Green Bell Pepper
- 2 tablespoons of Garlic
- 2 teaspoons of Salt
- 1 teaspoon of Black Pepper

- 4 ounces of Tomato Paste
- 1 16 ounce can of Tomatoes (crushed)
- 1 cup of your favorite BBQ Sauce
- ½ cup of your favorite Spicy BBQ Sauce
- 1 cup of Beef Stock
- 2 tablespoons of Worcestershire Sauce
- 1 tablespoon of Balsamic Vinegar
- 1 bag of Kidney Beans (soaked for 2 hours)
- ½ cup of Black Beans (soaked for 2 hours)

DIRECTIONS

- In a large stock pot or cast-iron skillet, brown the ground beef and sausage.
- Add in vegetables and cook until tender.
- Lower the heat and add chili powder, tomatoes, and tomato paste.
- Stir in both BBQ sauces and cook for 15 minutes.
- Add beer, beef broth, minced garlic, and Worcestershire sauce. Set aside.
- In a separate pot, add 3 ½ cups of water, salt, pepper, 2 teaspoons of seasoning salt, and beans.
- Cook for about 1 ½ hours until beans are tender and soft.
- Combine the chili sauce with ground beef to the beans.
- Cook for another 30 minutes on low heat.
- Serve with a little cheese on top and green onions.
- Enjoy!

Lil Mama's
Southern Black Eyed Peas

INGREDIENTS

- 2 cups of Black-Eyed Peas (dried)
- 10 oz Bacon chopped into pieces.
- 1 White Onion diced.
- 1 – 2 teaspoons of minced Garlic
- 4 cups of Chicken Broth

- ¼ teaspoons of Red Pepper Flakes
- ½ teaspoons of Seasoning Salt
- ½ teaspoon s of Black Pepper
- ½ cup of Okra (optional)

DIRECTIONS

- Rinse peas thoroughly under cool water and place them in a bowl, covering them with water. Soak for about 6 hours or overnight.

- Drain and rinse the peas again, then set them aside.

- In a large skillet over medium heat, cook bacon until crispy. Drain bacon on paper towels, leaving about 1 to 2 tablespoons of bacon fat in the pan.

- Add onions to the pan and cook until translucent. Then add garlic, chicken broth, and red pepper flakes.

- In a large pot, add all ingredients including the soaked black-eyed peas.

- Bring to a boil, then lower the heat to medium and cook for about 1 hour and 15 minutes or until the peas are tender.

- Serve over a bed of rice.

- Enjoy!

Lil Mama's Oxtails

INGREDIENTS

- 2.5 pounds of Oxtails
- Olive Oil to drizzle
- 2 tablespoons of Browning Gravy
- ¼ cup of Brown Sugar
- 1 jar of Jerk Seasoning
- 1 tablespoon of crushed Red Peppers
- 2 stalks of Celery
- 1 medium Red Bell Pepper

- 1 medium Green Bell Pepper
- 1 cup of Beef Broth
- 1 cup of Carrots
- 6 Red Skin Potatoes (cut)
- 1 cup of Red Potaoes
- 4 stalks of Green Onion
- ½ cup of Flour

DIRECTIONS

- Thoroughly clean the oxtails, discarding excess fat. Drizzle with olive oil and massage the oil into the oxtails.

- Coat the oxtails with flour and add them to a pan with oil. Brown the oxtails on each side.

- Cut up all the vegetables, then add the vegetables to the pressure cooker along with the oxtails.

- Add jerk seasoning, beef broth, gravy mix, and ½ cup of brown sugar to the pressure cooker.

- Set your pressure cooker for 1 hour and 45 minutes and release the steam.

- Add celery, potatoes, and carrots, then cook for another 15 minutes before releasing the pressure.

- Serve over a bed of rice.

- Enjoy!

Lil Mama's Southern Clam Chowder

INGREDIENTS

- 6 slices of Bacon (Hickory)
- 1 cup of diced Onions
- 3 cups of Red Skin Potatoes (about 3 large)
- 1 ½ tablespoons of Garlic
- 1 tablespoon of Lawry's seasoning salt
- ½ cup of Flour
- 8 ounces of Clam Juice
- 1 cup of Chicken Stock
- 1 cup of Whole Milk
- 1 ½ cups of Heavy Cream
- 3 cans of chopped Clam with Juice
- 1 tablespoon of fresh Thyme
- Fresh Black Pepper to taste
- Parsley for garnish

DIRECTIONS

- Cook bacon in a large soup pot until crisp.

  Add onions, potatoes, and garlic to the pot.
-
  Stir with bacon drippings, season with Lawry's seasoning salt and thyme.

- Cook until potatoes have softened, stirring to prevent burning.
-
  Sprinkle flour into the pot and stir to combine.

- Ensure flour is absorbed.

  Pour chicken broth and clam juice into the pot, scraping up
- the bottom as you stir.

- Bring to a simmer for 5 minutes to thicken.

- Stir in milk, cream, clams, and clam juice.

- Bring the chowder to a simmer and cook partially covered for 20 minutes.

- Stir often to prevent potatoes from sticking to the bottom.

- Pierce potatoes with a fork to check tenderness. If needed, cover and cook a few more minutes.

- Uncover and simmer for 5-7 more minutes once potatoes are tender.

- Serve with fresh chopped parsley for garnish and crackers on the side.

- Enjoy!

- Add onion, bell peppers, and chopped garlic.

- Cook for about 5 minutes, until slightly caramelized and softened.

- Add thyme and tomato paste.

- Pour in chicken broth and stir.

- Let the mixture reduce for about a minute.

- Remove skillet from burner and let cool.

Brown Gravy

- Beef Stock
- Beef Base Bouillon
- Corn Starch or Flour
- Worcestershire Sauce
- Garlic Powder
- Heavy Cream (optional if you want it

DIRECTIONS

- Add 1 ½ cup of beef stock or 4 bouillon cubes to a pot.

- If using bouillon cubes, add 1 cup of water.

- Add Worcestershire sauce and garlic powder.

- Bring to a boil.

- Slowly drizzle in cornstarch while whisking to prevent lumps.

- Bring the gravy back to a boil, then turn down the heat and le simmer for 4-5 minutes until thickened.

- Set aside one cup of gravy for the meatloaf mix and another cup for topping the meatloaf.

- In a large bowl, combine ground beef, eggs, and breadcrumbs.

- Once the onion mixture has cooled, combine it with the beef mixture (clean hands work best).

- Add 1 cup of brown gravy to the beef mixture.

- Line a sheet pan with aluminum foil and spray with cooking spray.

- Form the meat mixture into a loaf.

- Cook the meatloaf in a 350-degree oven for 50-55 minutes.

- Check the meatloaf after 50 minutes to see if it's cooked through, depending on the size and shape.

- If cooked all the way through, add another cup of brown gravy over the top.

- Serve with mashed potatoes.

- Enjoy!

Lil Mama's Southern Brown Gravy Meatloaf

INGREDIENTS

- 2 ½ pounds of Ground Beef or Turkey
- 1 tablespoon of Olive Oil
- 1 cup of diced Onions
- 1 small Red Bell Pepper (chopped in small pieces)
- 1 small Green Bell Pepper (chopped in small pieces)
- 1 ½ teaspoons of Kosher Salt
- ½ teaspoons Black Pepper
- ½ teaspoons Garlic Powder
- 1 ½ tablespoon of chopped Garlic
- 1 tablespoon of fresh chopped Thyme
- 1 tablespoon of Tomato Paste
- 1 ½ tablespoons of Worcestershire Sauce
- ½ cup of Chicken Broth
- 1 cup of Breadcrumbs
- 2 Eggs beaten.
- 2 cups of Brown Gravy

DIRECTIONS

- Preheat oven to 350 degrees.

- Heat oil in a skillet over medium heat.

About The Author

Tonja Stewart Nelson brings over 12 years of extensive culinary expertise to LIL Mama's Catering LLC. As the owner and head chef, she has honed her skills through years of hands-on experience and a deep-seated passion for cooking. Tonja's culinary journey began in her hometown of Mobile, Alabama, where she cultivated her craft under the guidance of her grandmother, mastering the secrets of Southern cuisine.

Throughout her career, Tonja has demonstrated a keen ability to blend traditional flavors with innovative techniques, resulting in dishes that are both delicious and visually captivating. Her commitment to excellence is evident in every aspect of her work, from ingredient selection to final presentation.

Tonja's dedication to her craft extends beyond the kitchen. She is deeply involved in her community, volunteering her time and talents to support various charitable endeavors. Her unwavering commitment to quality, creativity, and service excellence makes her a respected figure in the culinary industry and a driving force behind the success of LIL Mama's Catering LLC.

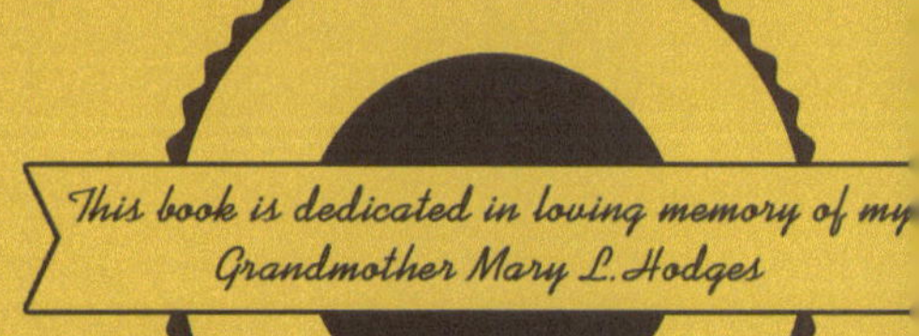

Thank you to everybody who has been there for me and who has believed in me on every step of the way.

From Tonja with love